Lee Hooper

An Investigation into the Relationship between India and Cows

Applying Beatson's Analytical Framework to a Structural-Functionalist Model

GRIN Verlag

Bibliografische Information der Deutschen Nationalbibliothek:

Die Deutsche Bibliothek verzeichnet diese Publikation in der Deutschen National-
bibliografie; detaillierte bibliografische Daten sind im Internet über http://dnb.d-
nb.de/ abrufbar.

Impressum:

Copyright © 2012 GRIN Verlag GmbH
Druck und Bindung: Books on Demand GmbH, Norderstedt Germany
ISBN: 978-3-656-51240-0

Dieses Buch bei GRIN:

http://www.grin.com/de/e-book/262263/an-investigation-into-the-relationship-
between-india-and-cows

GRIN - Your knowledge has value

Der GRIN Verlag publiziert seit 1998 wissenschaftliche Arbeiten von Studenten, Hochschullehrern und anderen Akademikern als eBook und gedrucktes Buch. Die Verlagswebsite www.grin.com ist die ideale Plattform zur Veröffentlichung von Hausarbeiten, Abschlussarbeiten, wissenschaftlichen Aufsätzen, Dissertationen und Fachbüchern.

Besuchen Sie uns im Internet:

http://www.grin.com/

http://www.facebook.com/grincom

http://www.twitter.com/grin_com

176.205 – Essay 2 (Topic 1)

An Investigation into the Relationship between India and Cows: Applying Beatson's Analytical Framework to a Structural-Functionalist Model

Approximate length – 2000 words

Submitted on 8th October

The relationship between human society and animals is composed of vast and inter-related examples scattered over every continent, which take on a multitude of different forms, some cohesive and some antagonistic. One such case, which highlights the mutual dependence between animal and human, is the case of cows in India. This essay will look to explore the various forms that the cow-human relationship has taken in India and show how each species has affected the other. In order to achieve this, Beatson's classificatory system of human-animal relationships will be outlined in relation to cows in India, and then analysed through a structural-functionalist model, which will highlight several of the key reasons for the usefulness of this relationship. By providing an overview of the cow-human relationship in this light, it is hoped that a holistic understanding is reached on why cows are an integral part of the Indian society.

In order to understand and make sense of the various ways that humans and animals interact, Beatson has outlined an analytical framework, whereby classifying seven different spheres of human-animal relationship (Beatson, 2012). These categories are; Nature, population, economy, politics, community, welfare, and culture. Throughout these seven spheres there is an interaction, which is based on reciprocal process of conditioning. In plain terms, there is an inherent two-way relationship between humans and animals, and while it can be argued that humans have greater impacts on the animal kingdom, there are times when the role is reversed and human life is somewhat dictated by the animals that surround them. Five of these spheres will now be elaborated on below, with each having examples pertaining specifically to the cow-human relationship in India.

The nature sphere is fundamentally defined by the boundary between human society, or civilization, and the wilderness (Beatson, 2012). To make it plain, it is the difference between the areas of land humans inhabit and call home and the areas that animals inhabit and call home. In most cases, those animals that are called wild typically live in the wilderness and those animals called domestic live within the confines of human society. In saying that, it should be mentioned that there is a divide between urban and rural areas and the types of animals that inhabit both. In the case of India, 72 percent of the population live in a rural environment (Turner, 1978). This means that the majority of interactions between cows and humans will occur in this setting. The main point of interest is that, unlike many farms in Western societies where cows are contained in paddocks, a large amount of cows in India roam free amongst the people. The significance of this is that the definition of what is a natural environment for a cow has progressed along a different path in India as compared with most other cultures, and because of this, the relationship between humans and cows has taken on a unique connection.

The population sphere encompasses six factors pertaining to human and cow statistical information; birth, death, migration, size, composition, and distribution (Beatson, 2012). Beatson also adds that there are four forms in which human demography has taken on animals; these are fatal contact, domestication, selective breeding and population explosion. In relation to this topic, domestication and population explosion are the most relevant. The domestication of cows is believed to have occurred approximately 8000-10,000 years ago, originating in the Indian and Middle East continents (Loftus et al, 1994). It is not surprising then that 30 percent of the earth's cow population lives in India, with a variety of different 'populations' of cows living in different areas. Turner notes that there are "city cows, country cows, coastal cows, high-altitude cows, trash-collector cows, Buddhist cows, Hindu cows, homeless cows, village cows, dancing cows, and licence-carrying cows", to name just a few (Turner, 2012, p. 10). Cows have been domesticated so much into Indian society that they take on a multitude of different roles.

In terms of the human population, India contains approximately a sixth of the world's population, at just over 1.2 billion people (World Bank, 2012). In many urban and semi urban areas there is overcrowding and a scarcity of land in rural areas (Singh & Singh, 1999). In conjunction with many rural people owning cows and the lack of land to raise them on, the expanding human population has encroached on the traditional living space of cows. In turn, the growing cow population has also affected the human population through the fact that cows are permitted to freely wander through cities and towns, defecating where they please and blocking railways and roads (Brym & Lie, 2007).

The economy sphere revolves around the production, exchange, and distribution of goods, alongside ownership and use values of cows and cow-related products (Beatson, 2012). As a large part of India is rural, there is a considerable dependency on livestock and a subsistence mode of living. Because of this, cows are intimately tied to the Indian economy on both macro and micro levels. For instance, since cows are able to reproduce and thus create more capital, as opposed to bulls and oxen, there is an economical benefit in keeping them alive, rather than slaughtering them for food (Harris, 1978). This example can be enlarged on the macro level as there is a large difference in the use of land and cost of production depending of the use of the cow (Harris, 1978). For instance, in America a large part of agricultural land is used to grow crops to feed livestock, which in turn feed humans. The cost of this economically, in terms on food product, fossil fuels, and labour, far exceeds the cost cows place on the India system, where cows graze on the remains of subsistence crops, and are not reared in order to be fat, plump, products of consumption. In addition, cows actually contribute to the economy by being a source of manual labour, having their manure used a fuel for cooking and as fertilizer, which saves on expensive commercial products (Bhasin, 2011).

The welfare sphere is composed of the actions and ideologies that manifest in caring behaviours and the wellbeing of both humans and cows (Beatson, 2012). One of the most striking examples of this is illustrated during the 1960's famine in India where people were emaciated while cows, a readily source of nutrition, where strolling throughout the community unbothered, and in fact competing with humans for nearby food such as fruit (Harris, 1978). Furthermore, in India there more than three thousand institutions called Gaushalas, which care for old and infirm cows. This demonstrates the degree that Indians will sacrifice their own wellbeing in order to ensure cows have a relatively high quality of life. The carry on effect from careful treatment of cows and the cultural practice of not consuming their flesh for food is that diseases such as bovine spongiform encephalopathy (mad cow disease) and Creutzfeldt-Jakob (a neurological disorder), that have been linked to beef consumption in several cases have not plagued the Indian population as much as other countries, where the health of cows have adversely affected the welfare of the humans who consumed them (Darshan et al, 2010).

The culture sphere is by far the most far-reaching of all the spheres, in relation to cows in India, and is intimately connected with all the above mentioned spheres (Beatson, 2012). The primary facet of this sphere in India is centred on the Hindu religion. The Hindu religion has a cow goddess called Kamadhenu, also known as Surabhi, which is said to be a protector of the Brahman, an upper class consisting of priests. This deity embodies qualities such as gentleness, compassion, and connection with nature, while in the Vedas, one of the main Hindu scripts, cows represent wealth and a prosperous life. In its basic form, "the cow is a symbol of health and abundance" as it provides sustenance in the form of its milk, which is made into yogurt and ghee, both integral parts of the Indian diet (Harris, 1978, p. 202). The Hindu law of *Ahimsa* prohibits the slaughter of cows, alongside the consumption of their flesh, and in accordance with the highly symbolic cultural nature of the cow, it is left alone to do as it pleases.

It must also be noted that the sacred role of the cow, along with the concurrent practices, only applies to Hindus, as Muslims and Christians have different values. Furthermore, even within the Hindu culture, there are exceptions, with the most notable being that those in the lower castes, such as the 'untouchables', are culturally accepted as eating the meat, and making products from its organs, provided that the cow has died naturally (Harris, 1978). In addition there are a variety of 'exceptions' to the slaughter of cows. Even though the Hindu's cannot directly kill cows, they can indirectly kill them by selling them onto people of other faiths, knowing that they will kill them, let the old and unhealthy starve to death on a tether, and put large wooden triangles around baby calves, so that they get kicked to death by the mother when trying to suckle milk. Harris (1978, p. 209) postulates that the "ecological realities" of rural life in India and the need to cull animals, may be a prominent factor in these types of instances.

To summarise all of the main points and underlying themes associated with Beatson's framework of cows in India, it can be said that the predominant rural setting of people and the uncontained setting for cows represent the nature sphere. The large populations of both cows and people living in India represent the population sphere. The manifestations of capitalist principles specific to India and use-values of cows represent the economic sphere. A strong sense of welfare for cows from Indians represents the welfare sphere. Finally, even though there are contradictions between human and cow needs that bend idealistic cultural norms of cow treatment, a strong religious ideology dictates the overall treatment of cows in the cultural sphere. A definition of structural-functionalism will now be outlined, followed by an analysis of how the relationships between cow and human in India can be interpreted in this theoretical framework.

Structural functionism is the theoretical position held within cultural anthropology that attempts to understand the relationship between the individual and society and in particular the conditions that places individuals in social roles (Barnard, 2000). It looks at the structural systems in place and the interaction between individuals due to these systems.

Structural functionalism is based primarily on the principles of universal function and functional unity (Ferraro & Andreatta, 2010). In simplistic terms this equates to every part of a culture having its own unique function and that every functional part of society can affect other parts as they are all interconnected. In structural functionalism the key question asked is how societies can remain stable and cohesive over time and what is needed for that to work (Harris, 2001). To answer this, social systems become the focal point of study. In particular the social institutions, norms, roles and statuses of individuals become the reflection upon which to examine cultural and society more in depth.

In relation to cows in India, one must ask what role these creatures have in society, along with how the relationships between humans and cows contribute to the function and structure of society. For instance, the worshiping and principle of not slaughtering the cow fit in with the environmental structure of the rural Indian (Nanda & Warms, 2011). By not killing the cow, it is able to provide labour, sustenance and fuel that fit in with the Indian economy, one of capitalist politics in a growing, yet impoverished country. What this means is that many rural Indians live on a subsistence type of diet and they have found, specific to their condition in India, that cows can provide greater use to human lives by being alive and producing goods rather than being on the dinner table.

Another reason why cows hold their unique place in society may also lay in the caste system (Fueller, 2004). Traditionally, those of high castes, such as Brahmans, were impelled to adhere to a strict vegetarian diet. Consequently, the practice of vegetarianism came with a higher status, especially as the slaughtering of animals was confined to the lowest of castes, such as 'the untouchables'. Therefore, it can be postulated that the caste system structure of segregation through dietary choice, may have influenced the function of cows in India, as status was correlated with vegetarianism, and hence, not killing cows. Lastly, the close connection with cows may help to form part of a cohesive community through the symbolism attached to the cow by Hindu mythology. By having a common entity to place attention upon, a sense of kinship is created, which will help to unify elements of the country and provide stability (Layton, 1997).

In summary, by providing a detailed overview of how the cow-human relationship fits into various spheres of Beatson's analytical framework, a holistic picture is gained on the unique situation in Indian culture. Beatson's framework allows a simple categorisation of many of the various ways that humans and animals interact. By applying this framework to a structural-functionalist approach, these relationships can then be expanded on to see how and why they are necessary elements of the Indian society. In conclusion, while these approaches fail to account for individual action, as they are both generalised theories, and structural-functionalism focus is fairly limited to the mechanics of society, they do provide a useful method for understanding certain areas of society, particularly the role that cows play in India. It is hoped that by combining these two theories together, a more complex appreciation is gained of the cows place in India.

References

Barnard, A. (2000). *History and theory in anthropology.* Cambridge: Cambridge University Press.

Beatson, P. (2012). *Mapping human-animal relations: An analytical framework.* Palmerston North, New Zealand: School of People, Environment, and Planning.

Bhasin, V. (2011). Pastoralists of the Himalayas. *Journal of Human Ecology, 33*(3), 147-177.

Brym, R., & Lie, J. (2007). *Sociology: Your compass for a new world* (3rd ed). Belmont, CA: Thompson Wadesworth.

Darshan, S., Krewski, D., Karyakina, N., & Tyshenko, M. G. (2010). Preventive risk management strategies for bovine spongiform encephalopathy and variant Creutzfeldt-Jakob disease in India. *International Journal of Risk Assessment & Management, 14*(3-4), 239-253.

Ferraro, G., & Andreatta, S. (2010). *Cultural anthropology: An applied perspective, 8th ed.* U.S.A: Wadsworth, Cengage Learning.

Fueller, C. J. (2004). *The camphor flame: Popular Hinduism and society in India* (2nd ed). Princeton, NJ: Princeton University Press.

Harris, M. (1978). India's sacred cows. *Human Nature*

Harris, M. (2001). *The rise of anthropological theory: A history of theories of culture.* U.S.A: AltaMira Press.

Layton, R. (1997). An introduction to theory in anthropology. Cambridge, UK: Cambridge University Press.

Loftus, R. T., MacHugh, D. E., Bradley, D. G., Sharp, P. M., & Cunningham, P. (1994). Evidence for Two Independent Domestications of Cattle. *Proceedings Of The National Academy Of Sciences Of The United States Of America, 91*(7), 2757-2761.

Nanda, S., & Warms, R. (2011). *Cultural anthropology* (11th ed). Belmont, CA: Wadsworth Publishing.

Ramkumar, S., Rao, S. V. N., & Waldie, K. (2004). Dairy cattle rearing by landless rural women in pondicherry: A path to empowerment. *Indian Journal of Gender Studies, 11*(2), 205-222.

Singh, U.P., & Singh, A.K. (1999). *Human ecology and development in India.* Daryaganj, New Delhi: APH Publishing.

Turner, E. (2012). 'Til the cows come home. *This Land, 3*(12), 10.

World Bank. (2012). *World development indicators and global development finance.* Retrieved from http://www.google.co.nz/publicdata/explore?ds=d5bncppjof8f9_&met_y=sp_pop_totl&idim=country:IND&dl=en&hl=en&q=india+population